MW01387816

Keto
NINJA CREAMi
Recipes

Amazingly Delicious Frozen Treats for your Low-Carb, High-Fat Life!

Anna GAINES

Copyright © 2022 A. GAINES - All rights reserved.

No part of this publication may be reproduced, distributed, or transmitted in any form or by any means, including photocopying, recording, or other electronic or mechanical methods, without the prior written permission of the author.

Recipes are provided for private and personal use only.

The text and recipes should not be considered a substitute for professional medical advice. The author shall not be held liable for any adverse effects arising from the use of the information and recipes contained herein. The reader should consult a qualified medical professional before starting any new health or diet program.

Table of Contents

When we go to the store freezers, there are not enough keto ice cream options available. And that makes us sad. So, the best option is to try to make your own frozen treats. And that's an exercise in frustration. Mostly because recipes for keto frozen treats are not easily found in the cookbooks market.

Unfortunately, traditional ice cream—mostly made with cow's milk and sugar—is not so healthy; but despite the health risks, people don't want to give it up and who can blame them? Good ice cream is delicious! Judging by the attention paid to low-fat and fat-free ice creams on sale in store freezers.

You could be forgiven for thinking that the big bad monster in ice cream is fat. But scientific research shows unequivocally that the real villain of traditional ice cream is not fat, but sugar.

Now you can eat fantastic frozen treats that will help, not hurt, your health. Even if it wasn't a search for healthy frozen treats that brought you here, why eat the usual frozen treats when you can have a super healthy option that tastes even better?

These recipes support our health and body fat goals by providing nutrient rich protein and fat, while being extremely low in carbs and full of vitamins and minerals.

Each one of them is very delicious. Enjoy!

About the Recipes

When most recipes say they are sugar-free, it really means that they do not contain regular refined white sugar. Typically, white sugar is replaced with honey, agave, coconut sugar, maple syrup, brown sugar or, increasingly, dried fruit like dates. The point is that our bodies react to all of these alternatives in essentially the same way as they react to refined white sugar. For all intents and purposes, sugar is sugar as far as our bodies are concerned, and our bodies can't tell the difference between refined white sugar and the other products I mentioned.

When I say my recipes are sugar free, I mean that they are free of any added sugar, or anything that makes your body react the same way as refined white sugar. If your goal is to lose fat, you'll do much better with recipes that don't contain refined white sugar or the commonly used substitutes I mentioned above.

For those of you who are wondering about fruit, it is true that it does contain sugar. That's why I only use whole fruit—never juice—and focus on the least sugary and most nutritionally dense fruits: berries and some citrus. The fiber in whole fruit helps control the effect of dietary sugar on blood sugar, and our bodies absorb natural sugars more slowly. We are less likely to experience a blood sugar spike, which we want to avoid. Fiber is also good for us.

Yet, despite the fiber, if fat loss is your main goal, you shouldn't eat too much fruit-based frozen treats at once. Fortunately, my frozen treats recipes are very filling and I'm happy with one or two small scoops. When I used to eat regular ice cream, I could swallow a whole tub of it without even thinking about it. It's the sugar that does it to you.

Speaking of eating frozen treats, and while these ice creams are much better for us than traditional ice cream, remember that they should be considered treats. An organism cannot feed itself on ice cream alone, even the healthiest ones. For optimal health and body fat control, nutrient-dense protein and healthy fats from whole foods must be the foundation of a ketogenic diet. These frozen treats contain protein and are full of healthy fats. Eat them as a dessert, not as a main course!

As with any other recipe, the flavor and nutritional quality of frozen treats depends to a large extent on the quality of the ingredients used. If you are going to put in the effort to make your own frozen treats, I thoroughly recommend using the best ingredients you can get your hands on.

All recipes are free of sugar, grains, gluten, eggs, and soy. Most can be easily modified to accommodate folks who are dairy free. Safe for Diabetics.

Let the frozen treats making begin!

ICE CREAMS

Vanilla Ice Cream

INGREDIENTS

- 1½ cups almond milk
- 1 whole vanilla pod, split lengthwise, seeds scraped out
- 3½ oz xylitol
- 1 tsp sea salt
- 1 cup heavy cream
- 1½ cups thick coconut milk
- 1 tsp vanilla extract
- 1 tsp guar gum

INSTRUCTIONS

In a medium saucepan, heat the almond milk, vanilla seeds and bean, xylitol, sea salt and cream until the mixture begins to boil.

Simmer for one minute, then remove from heat, cover and let steep for one hour.

Pour the vanilla-infused milk through a strainer to remove the vanilla bean.

Place the thick coconut milk in a blender with the vanilla-infused milk and vanilla extract and blend for 10 seconds.

Put the blender on low speed, and while it is running, add the guar gum by tapping it through the opening in the lid, and blend for 30 seconds.

Transfer the mixture to a Ninja CREAMi Dessert Tub.

Cover the tub with a lid and freeze for 24 hours.

After freezing, remove the lid from the tub and place it in the Outer Bowl. Install the Creamerizer Paddle.

Place the Outer Bowl on the motor base and lock it.

Turn **ON** the NINJA CREAMi and press the **ICE CREAM** button.

Once the program is finished, release the Outer Bowl from the motor base and remove the lid.

Serve the ice cream with the topping of your choice and enjoy!

Dark Chocolate Ice Cream

INGREDIENTS

- 1½ cups hemp milk
- ½ cup heavy cream
- 5¼ oz xylitol
- ½ tsp sea salt
- 1¼ oz raw unsweetened cocoa powder
- 2 oz 100% cocoa dark chocolate chopped
- 1½ cups thick coconut milk
- 1 tsp vanilla extract
- ½ tsp guar gum

INSTRUCTIONS

Place the hemp milk, cream, xylitol, sea salt and cocoa powder in a saucepan over medium heat and whisk until the cocoa powder is fully incorporated.

Bring to a boil, reduce heat and simmer for one minute, whisking constantly.

Remove the saucepan from the heat and stir in the chopped chocolate.

Let cool, stirring well from time to time.

Place the thick coconut milk and vanilla extract in the blender, add the cooled chocolate cream and blend for 10 seconds.

Put the blender on low speed and, while it is running, add the guar gum by tapping it through the opening in the lid, and blend for 30 seconds.

Transfer the mixture to a Ninja CREAMi Dessert Tub.

Cover the tub with a lid and freeze for 24 hours.

After freezing, remove the lid from the tub and place it in the Outer Bowl. Install the Creamerizer Paddle.

Place the Outer Bowl on the motor base and lock it.

Turn **ON** the NINJA CREAMi and press the **ICE CREAM** button.

Once the program is finished, release the Outer Bowl from the motor base and remove the lid.

Serve the ice cream with the topping of your choice and enjoy!

Avocado Ice Cream

INGREDIENTS

- 1 cup almond milk
- ½ cup heavy cream
- 4 oz sour cream
- 3½ oz xylitol
- ½ tsp sea salt
- 1 tbsp white wine vinegar
- 2 tbsp vegetable glycerin
- 12 oz avocado flesh
- 1 tsp guar gum

INSTRUCTIONS

Place the almond milk, cream, sour cream, xylitol, sea salt, white wine vinegar, and vegetable glycerin in a blender and blend for 10 seconds.

With the blender running on low speed, add the avocado flesh and guar gum through the hole in the blender lid and blend until smooth. The cream will be very thick and you may need to stop the blender and scrape down the sides once or twice.

Transfer the mixture to a Ninja CREAMi Dessert Tub.

Cover the tub with a lid and freeze for 24 hours.

After freezing, remove the lid from the tub and place it in the Outer Bowl. Install the Creamerizer Paddle.

Place the Outer Bowl on the motor base and lock it.

Turn **ON** the NINJA CREAMi and press the **ICE CREAM** button.

Once the program is finished, release the Outer Bowl from the motor base and remove the lid.

Serve the ice cream with the topping of your choice and enjoy!

Triple Coconut Ice Cream

INGREDIENTS

- 4 oz flaked coconut, unsweetened
- 1½ cups thick coconut milk
- 1¼ cup thin coconut milk
- 3½ oz xylitol
- ¾ cup heavy cream
- 1 tsp sea salt
- ½ tsp rum
- 1 tsp guar gum

INSTRUCTIONS

In Spread the coconut on a baking sheet and toast under a broiler until lightly browned. Browning happens very quickly—do not walk away! Remove from under the broiler and leave to cool. Store in the freezer.

Place half (2 oz) of the toasted coconut, the thick and thin coconut-milk, xylitol, cream, sea salt, and rum in a pan and warm over medium heat until it just comes to the boil. Remove from the heat and leave to cool for 15 minutes.

Pour the coconut mixture into a blender and blend for 30 seconds. It will NOT be smooth. DO NOT CONTINUE TO BLEND TO GET TO SMOOTH.

Turn the blender to low speed, and while the blender is running, add the guar gum by tapping it through the opening in the lid, and blend for 30 seconds.

Transfer the mixture to a Ninja CREAMi Dessert Tub.

Cover the tub with a lid and freeze for 24 hours.

After freezing, remove the lid from the tub and add the remaining half (2 oz) toasted frozen coconut flakes. Place the tub in the Outer Bowl. Install the Creamerizer Paddle.

Place the Outer Bowl on the motor base and lock it.

Turn **ON** the NINJA CREAMi and press the **ICE CREAM** button.

Once the program is finished, release the Outer Bowl from the motor base and remove the lid.

Serve the ice cream with the topping of your choice and enjoy!

Dirty Chai Ice Cream

INGREDIENTS

- 1¾ cups thin coconut milk
- 3½ oz xylitol
- 4 Chai tea bags
- 1¾ cups heavy cream
- 1½ tbsp espresso powder
- ½ tsp sea salt
- 1 tsp guar gum

INSTRUCTIONS

Warm the coconut milk and xylitol in a medium saucepan until it just starts to boil. Remove from the heat, add the chai tea bags, stir well and leave for an hour to steep.

Pour the chai-infused milk through a sieve to remove the tea bags, and then return the infused milk to the saucepan over a low heat.

Add the cream, espresso powder, and salt and stir well until the espresso powder is dissolved, and then remove from the heat.

Carefully pour the espresso chai mixture into a blender and blend for 10 seconds.

Turn the blender to low speed, and while the blender is running, add the guar gum by tapping it through the opening in the lid, and blend for 30 seconds.

Transfer the mixture to a Ninja CREAMi Dessert Tub.

Cover the tub with a lid and freeze for 24 hours.

After freezing, remove the lid from the tub and place it in the Outer Bowl. Install the Creamerizer Paddle.

Place the Outer Bowl on the motor base and lock it.

Turn **ON** the NINJA CREAMi and press the **ICE CREAM** button.

Once the program is finished, release the Outer Bowl from the motor base and remove the lid.

Serve the ice cream with the topping of your choice and enjoy!

Cinnamon Ice Cream

INGREDIENTS

- 1½ cup almond milk, unsweetened vanilla
- 1 cup heavy cream
- 3½ oz xylitol
- ½ tsp sea salt
- 1 cup thick coconut milk
- 1½ tsp ground cinnamon
- ¼ tsp vanilla extract
- 1 tsp guar gum

INSTRUCTIONS

In Place the almond milk, cream, xylitol, salt, coconut milk, ground cinnamon and vanilla extract in a blender and blend for 10 seconds.

Turn the blender to low speed and while it is running, add the guar gum by tapping it through the opening in the lid and blend for 30 seconds.

Transfer the mixture to a Ninja CREAMi Dessert Tub.

Cover the tub with a lid and freeze for 24 hours.

After freezing, remove the lid from the tub and place it in the Outer Bowl. Install the Creamerizer Paddle.

Place the Outer Bowl on the motor base and lock it.

Turn **ON** the NINJA CREAMi and press the **ICE CREAM** button.

Once the program is finished, release the Outer Bowl from the motor base and remove the lid.

Serve the ice cream with the topping of your choice and enjoy!

Peanut Butter Ice Cream

- 2 cups hemp milk, unsweetened
- ¾ cup smooth natural unsweetened peanut butter
- 6¼ oz xylitol
- ½ tsp sea salt
- ½ cup heavy cream
- ¼ tsp vanilla extract
- ½ tsp guar gum

INSTRUCTIONS

Place the hemp milk, peanut butter, xylitol, salt, cream, and vanilla extract into a blender and blend for 10 seconds.

Turn the blender to low speed, and while the blender is running, add the guar gum by tapping it through the opening in the lid, and blend for 30 seconds.

Transfer the mixture to a Ninja CREAMi Dessert Tub.

Cover the tub with a lid and freeze for 24 hours.

After freezing, remove the lid from the tub and place it in the Outer Bowl. Install the Creamerizer Paddle.

Place the Outer Bowl on the motor base and lock it.

Turn **ON** the NINJA CREAMi and press the **ICE CREAM** button.

Once the program is finished, release the Outer Bowl from the motor base and remove the lid.

Serve the ice cream with the topping of your choice and enjoy!

Orange Ice Cream

INGREDIENTS

- Zest of 4 oranges
- 1 cup almond milk
- ½ cup heavy cream
- 3½ oz xylitol
- ½ tsp sea salt
- 1 cup thick coconut milk
- ½ tsp vanilla extract
- 1 tsp orange extract
- 1 tsp guar gum

INSTRUCTIONS

Zest the oranges directly into a small saucepan.

Add the almond milk, cream, xylitol, and salt to the saucepan with the zest, stir well, and bring just to the boil. Remove from the heat, cover, and leave to cool.

Pass the orange milk through a sieve to remove the zest. Discard the zest.

Place the orange milk in a blender with the coconut milk, vanilla extract, and orange extract, and blend for 10 seconds.

Turn the blender to low speed, and while the blender is running, add the guar gum by tapping it through the opening in the lid, and blend for 30 seconds.

Transfer the mixture to a Ninja CREAMi Dessert Tub.

Cover the tub with a lid and freeze for 24 hours.

After freezing, remove the lid from the tub and place it in the Outer Bowl. Install the Creamerizer Paddle.

Place the Outer Bowl on the motor base and lock it.

Turn **ON** the NINJA CREAMi and press the **ICE CREAM** button.

Once the program is finished, release the Outer Bowl from the motor base and remove the lid.

Serve the ice cream with the topping of your choice and enjoy!

Blueberry Ice Cream

INGREDIENTS

- ¾ cup almond milk
- 3½ oz xylitol
- ½ tsp sea salt
- 1½ tsp cinnamon extract
- ¾ cup heavy cream
- 8 oz fresh blueberries
- ½ cups thick coconut milk
- 4 oz cream cheese
- 1 tsp guar gum

INSTRUCTIONS

Warm the almond milk, xylitol, salt, cinnamon extract, and cream in a medium saucepan until it just starts to boil.

Remove from the heat and carefully pour into a blender.

Immediately add the fresh blueberries and blend until smooth.

Add the thick coconut milk and cream cheese to the warm blueberry cream and blend on low until completely smooth.

With the blender still on low speed, and while the blender is running, add the guar gum by tapping it through the opening in the lid, and blend for 30 seconds.

Transfer the mixture to a Ninja CREAMi Dessert Tub.

Cover the tub with a lid and freeze for 24 hours.

After freezing, remove the lid from the tub and place it in the Outer Bowl. Install the Creamerizer Paddle.

Place the Outer Bowl on the motor base and lock it.

Turn **ON** the NINJA CREAMi and press the **ICE CREAM** button.

Once the program is finished, release the Outer Bowl from the motor base and remove the lid.

Serve the ice cream with the topping of your choice and enjoy!

Nutty Ice Cream

INGREDIENTS

- 4 oz toasted hazelnuts
- 1 cup almond milk
- 1 cup heavy cream
- 3½ oz xylitol
- 2 tsp glycerin
- ½ tsp sea salt
- 2 oz 100% cocoa solids chocolate, chopped
- 1 cup thick coconut milk
- 1 tsp vanilla extract
- 1 tsp guar gum

INSTRUCTIONS

Warm the hazelnuts, almond milk, cream, xylitol, glycerin and salt in a medium saucepan until it just starts to boil. Remove from the heat, cover and leave for an hour to steep. Soaking your nuts is important.

Rewarm the saucepan over a low heat, and once warm add the chopped chocolate and stir until completely melted. Carefully pour the warm chocolate hazelnut cream into a blender, add the thick coconut milk and vanilla extract and blend on high until smooth.

Turn the blender to low speed, and while the blender is running, add the guar gum by tapping it through the opening in the lid, and blend for 30 seconds.

Transfer the mixture to a Ninja CREAMi Dessert Tub.

Cover the tub with a lid and freeze for 24 hours.

After freezing, remove the lid from the tub and place it in the Outer Bowl. Install the Creamerizer Paddle.

Place the Outer Bowl on the motor base and lock it.

Turn **ON** the NINJA CREAMi and press the **ICE CREAM** button.

Once the program is finished, release the Outer Bowl from the motor base and remove the lid.

Serve the ice cream with the topping of your choice and enjoy!

Root Beer Float Ice Cream

INGREDIENTS

- 1 cup thick coconut milk
- 1¼ cup almond milk
- ½ cup heavy cream
- ¼ cup avocado oil
- 3½ oz xylitol
- ½ tsp sea salt
- 1 tsp vanilla extract
- 4 tsp root beer extract
- 1 tsp guar gum

INSTRUCTIONS

Place all ingredients except the guar gum in a blender and blend for 10 seconds.

Turn the blender to low speed, and while the blender is running, add the guar gum by tapping it through the opening in the lid, and blend for 30 seconds.

Transfer the mixture to a Ninja CREAMi Dessert Tub.

Cover the tub with a lid and freeze for 24 hours.

After freezing, remove the lid from the tub and place it in the Outer Bowl. Install the Creamerizer Paddle.

Place the Outer Bowl on the motor base and lock it.

Turn **ON** the NINJA CREAMi and press the **ICE CREAM** button.

Once the program is finished, release the Outer Bowl from the motor base and remove the lid.

Serve the ice cream with the topping of your choice and enjoy!

Basil Ice Cream

INGREDIENTS

- 1 cup heavy cream
- ¾ cup unsweetened almond milk
- 4 oz xylitol
- ¾ tsp sea salt
- 2 oz fresh basil leaves
- ½ cup thick coconut milk
- 8 oz ricotta cheese
- 1 tbsp lemon juice
- 1 tsp guar gum

INSTRUCTIONS

Warm the cream, almond milk, xylitol, salt, and basil leaves in a medium saucepan until it just starts to boil. Remove from the heat, cover and leave for an hour to steep.

Pour the basil-infused milk through a sieve to remove the leaves. Press down hard on the leaves to extract as much flavor as possible. DO NOT DISCARD THE LEAVES.

Place the thick coconut milk, ricotta, and lemon juice in a blender with the strained basil-infused milk, and blend on low for 30 seconds. Add 1 tablespoon of the soggy basil leaves from earlier and blend until the custard is flecked with little basil pieces.

With the blender still on low speed, and while the blender is running, add the guar gum by tapping it through the opening in the lid, and blend for 30 seconds.

Transfer the mixture to a Ninja CREAMi Dessert Tub.

Cover the tub with a lid and freeze for 24 hours.

After freezing, remove the lid from the tub and place it in the Outer Bowl. Install the Creamerizer Paddle.

Place the Outer Bowl on the motor base and lock it.

Turn **ON** the NINJA CREAMi and press the **ICE CREAM** button.

Once the program is finished, release the Outer Bowl from the motor base and remove the lid.

Serve the ice cream with the topping of your choice and enjoy!

Rocky Road Ice Cream

INGREDIENTS

- 1½ cups hemp milk unsweetened
- 1 cup heavy cream
- 4½ oz xylitol
- ½ tsp sea salt
- 1¼ oz raw unsweetened cocoa powder
- 1 cup thick coconut milk
- 1 tsp vanilla extract
- 1 tsp guar gum
- 3 oz walnuts toasted and chopped
- 4 tbsp Sugar-free Mini Marshmallows

INSTRUCTIONS

Place the hemp milk, cream, xylitol, salt, and cocoa powder in a saucepan over medium heat and whisk until the cocoa powder is completely mixed in. Bring to the boil, reduce the heat, and simmer for 1 minute, whisking constantly.

Leave to cool stirring well occasionally.

Place the thick coconut milk and vanilla extract in the blender, add the cooled chocolate custard and blend for 10 seconds.

Turn the blender to low speed, and while the blender is running, add the guar gum by tapping it through the opening in the lid, and blend for 30 seconds.

Transfer the mixture to a Ninja CREAMi Dessert Tub.

Cover the tub with a lid and freeze for 24 hours.

After freezing, remove the lid from the tub and place it in the Outer Bowl. Install the Creamerizer Paddle.

Place the Outer Bowl on the motor base and lock it.

Turn **ON** the NINJA CREAMi and press the **ICE CREAM** button.

Once it is done, use a spoon to make a hole 1½ inch wide in the center that reaches the bottom of the tub.

Add the walnuts and marshmallows to the hole and press the **MIX-IN** button.

Once the program is finished, release the Outer Bowl from the motor base and remove the lid.

Serve the ice cream with the topping of your choice and enjoy!

Bacon Ice Cream

INGREDIENTS

- 1 cup heavy cream
- 1¼ cups hemp milk, unsweetened
- 4 oz xylitol
- 2½ tbsp caramel extract
- 1 tsp sea salt
- ½ cup thick coconut milk
- ¼ cup avocado oil
- 2 oz full-fat cream cheese
- 1 tsp guar gum
- 8 oz bacon, cooked (but NOT hard and crispy), chopped

INSTRUCTIONS

Warm the cream, hemp milk, xylitol, caramel extract, and salt in a medium saucepan until it just starts to boil. Simmer for 1 minute and then remove from the heat.

Place the thick coconut milk, avocado oil, and cream cheese in a blender with the warm caramel cream, and blend on low for 30 seconds.

With the blender on low speed, and while the blender is running, add the guar gum by tapping it through the opening in the lid, and blend for 30 seconds.

Transfer the mixture to a Ninja CREAMi Dessert Tub.

Cover the tub with a lid and freeze for 24 hours.

After freezing, remove the lid from the tub and place it in the Outer Bowl. Install the Creamerizer Paddle.

Place the Outer Bowl on the motor base and lock it.

Turn **ON** the NINJA CREAMi and press the **ICE CREAM** button.

Once it is done, use a spoon to make a hole 1½ inch wide in the center that reaches the bottom of the tub.

Add the chopped bacon to the hole and press the **MIX-IN** button.

Once the program is finished, release the Outer Bowl from the motor base and remove the lid.

Serve the ice cream with the topping of your choice and enjoy!

Pecan Ice Cream

INGREDIENTS

- 1 scoop Vanilla Protein Powder
- 1 cup almond milk
- 2 tablespoons unsalted butter, melted
- ¼ teaspoon salt
- 3 oz xylitol
- ¼ teaspoon maple extract
- ½ cup pecan halves
- ¼ teaspoon guar gum

INSTRUCTIONS

Place all ingredients except the pecans and the guar gum in a blender and blend for 10 seconds.

Turn the blender to low speed, and while the blender is running, add the guar gum by tapping it through the opening in the lid, and blend for 30 seconds.

Combine all the ingredients in a blender and blend until fully mixed and smooth in consistency.

Transfer the mixture to a Ninja CREAMi Dessert Tub.

Cover the tub with a lid and freeze for 24 hours.

After freezing, remove the lid from the tub and place it in the Outer Bowl. Install the Creamerizer Paddle.

Place the Outer Bowl on the motor base and lock it.

Turn **ON** the NINJA CREAMi and press the **LITE ICE CREAM** button.

Once it is done, use a spoon to make a hole 1½ inch wide in the center that reaches the bottom of the tub.

Add the pecans to the hole and press the **MIX-IN** button.

Once the program is finished, release the Outer Bowl from the motor base and remove the lid.

Serve the ice cream with the topping of your choice and enjoy!

SHAKES

Chocolate Shake

INGREDIENTS

- 1½ cups Dark Chocolate Ice Cream
- ½ cup unsweetened chocolate almond milk

INSTRUCTIONS

In a Ninja CREAMi Dessert Tub, place the chocolate ice cream and the chocolate almond milk.

Place the tub in the Outer Bowl. Install the Creamerizer Paddle.

Place the Outer Bowl on the motor base and lock it.

Turn **ON** the NINJA CREAMi and press the **MILKSHAKE** button.

Once the program is finished, release the Outer Bowl from the motor base and remove the lid.

Serve the shake with the topping of your choice and enjoy!

Oreo Shake

INGREDIENTS

- 1½ cups Vanilla Ice Cream
- ¼ cup peanut butter
- ¼ cup Mini Oreo cookies

INSTRUCTIONS

In a Ninja CREAMi Dessert Tub, place the vanilla ice cream and scoop a hole in the middle that goes to the bottom.

Put the peanut butter and Oreo in the hole that you created.

Place the tub in the Outer Bowl. Install the Creamerizer Paddle.

Place the Outer Bowl on the motor base and lock it.

Turn **ON** the NINJA CREAMi and press the **MILKSHAKE** button.

Once the program is finished, release the Outer Bowl from the motor base and remove the lid.

Serve the shake with the topping of your choice and enjoy!

Mint Chocolate Shake

INGREDIENTS

- 1 cup Vanilla Ice Cream
- ⅓ cup unsweetened almond milk
- 2 tsp unsweetened cocoa powder
- ¼ tsp peppermint extract
- ¼ tsp dried mint leaves

INSTRUCTIONS

Place all ingredients in a Ninja CREAMi Dessert Tub.

Place the tub in the Outer Bowl. Install the Creamerizer Paddle.

Place the Outer Bowl on the motor base and lock it.

Turn **ON** the NINJA CREAMi and press the **MILKSHAKE** button.

Once the program is finished, release the Outer Bowl from the motor base and remove the lid.

Serve the shake with the topping of your choice and enjoy!

Cinnamon Shake

- 1 cup Vanilla Ice Cream
- ⅓ cup unsweetened almond milk
- 1 tsp vanilla extract
- ¼ tsp ground cinnamon
- ¼ tsp ground nutmeg
- Pinch of sea salt

INSTRUCTIONS

Place all ingredients in a Ninja CREAMi Dessert Tub.

Place the tub in the Outer Bowl. Install the Creamerizer Paddle.

Place the Outer Bowl on the motor base and lock it.

Turn **ON** the NINJA CREAMi and press the **MILKSHAKE** button.

Once the program is finished, release the Outer Bowl from the motor base and remove the lid.

Serve the shake with the topping of your choice and enjoy!

Vanilla Shake

INGREDIENTS

- 1 scoop vanilla protein powder
- ½ tsp vanilla extract
- ¼ cup heavy cream
- ½ cup unsweetened almond milk

INSTRUCTIONS

Place all ingredients in a Ninja CREAMi Dessert Tub.

Place the tub in the Outer Bowl. Install the Creamerizer Paddle.

Place the Outer Bowl on the motor base and lock it.

Turn **ON** the NINJA CREAMi and press the **MILKSHAKE** button.

Once the program is finished, release the Outer Bowl from the motor base and remove the lid.

Serve the shake with the topping of your choice and enjoy!

Peanut Butter Shake

INGREDIENTS

- ¼ cup heavy cream
- ⅓ cup strawberries
- 3 tbsp natural peanut butter
- ½ cup unsweetened almond milk
- 1 tsp pure vanilla extract

INSTRUCTIONS

Place all ingredients in a Ninja CREAMi Dessert Tub.

Place the tub in the Outer Bowl. Install the Creamerizer Paddle.

Place the Outer Bowl on the motor base and lock it.

Turn **ON** the NINJA CREAMi and press the **MILKSHAKE** button.

Once the program is finished, release the Outer Bowl from the motor base and remove the lid.

Serve the shake with the topping of your choice and enjoy!

Mocha Shake

INGREDIENTS

- ½ cup unsweetened almond milk
- ¼ cup heavy cream
- 1½ tbsp MTC oil
- 2 tbsp instant coffee
- 1½ tbsp cocoa powder

INSTRUCTIONS

Place all ingredients in a Ninja CREAMi Dessert Tub.

Place the tub in the Outer Bowl. Install the Creamerizer Paddle.

Place the Outer Bowl on the motor base and lock it.

Turn **ON** the NINJA CREAMi and press the **MILKSHAKE** button.

Once the program is finished, release the Outer Bowl from the motor base and remove the lid.

Serve the shake with the topping of your choice and enjoy!

Blueberry Shake

INGREDIENTS

- ⅓ cup blueberries
- ⅔ cup unsweetened almond milk
- 1 scoop vanilla protein powder
- 2 tbsp natural almond butter
- ¼ tsp ground cinnamon

INSTRUCTIONS

Place all ingredients in a Ninja CREAMi Dessert Tub.

Place the tub in the Outer Bowl. Install the Creamerizer Paddle.

Place the Outer Bowl on the motor base and lock it.

Turn **ON** the NINJA CREAMi and press the **MILKSHAKE** button.

Once the program is finished, release the Outer Bowl from the motor base and remove the lid.

Serve the shake with the topping of your choice and enjoy!

Raspberry-Chocolate Shake

INGREDIENTS

- ¼ cup heavy cream
- ⅓ cup raspberries
- 1 scoop chocolate protein powder
- 1 tbsp cocoa powder
- ½ cup unsweetened almond milk

INSTRUCTIONS

Place all ingredients in a Ninja CREAMi Dessert Tub.

Place the tub in the Outer Bowl. Install the Creamerizer Paddle.

Place the Outer Bowl on the motor base and lock it.

Turn **ON** the NINJA CREAMi and press the **MILKSHAKE** button.

Once the program is finished, release the Outer Bowl from the motor base and remove the lid.

Serve the shake with the topping of your choice and enjoy!

SMOOTHIE BOWLS

Protein Smoothie Bowl

INGREDIENTS

- 10 ounces mixed berries
- ½ cup thick coconut milk
- 1 scoop protein powder
- 1 tablespoon peanut butter
- ½ cup unsweetened almond milk

INSTRUCTIONS

In a high-speed blender, place all ingredients and blend until smooth.

Transfer the mixture to a Ninja CREAMi Dessert Tub.

Cover the tub with a lid and freeze for 24 hours.

After freezing, remove the lid from the tub and place it in the Outer Bowl. Install the Creamerizer Paddle.

Place the Outer Bowl on the motor base and lock it.

Turn **ON** the NINJA CREAMi and press the **SMOOTHIE BOWL** button.

Once the program is finished, release the Outer Bowl from the motor base and remove the lid.

Serve the smoothie bowl with the topping of your choice and enjoy!

Ultimate Smoothie Bowl

INGREDIENTS

- 1 scoop vanilla protein powder
- ½ medium avocado
- ⅓ cup mixed berries
- 1 tbsp Açaí powder
- ¾ cup unsweetened almond milk

INSTRUCTIONS

In a high-speed blender, place all ingredients and blend until smooth.

Transfer the mixture to a Ninja CREAMi Dessert Tub.

Cover the tub with a lid and freeze for 24 hours.

After freezing, remove the lid from the tub and place it in the Outer Bowl. Install the Creamerizer Paddle.

Place the Outer Bowl on the motor base and lock it.

Turn **ON** the NINJA CREAMi and press the **SMOOTHIE BOWL** button.

Once the program is finished, release the Outer Bowl from the motor base and remove the lid.

Serve the smoothie bowl with the topping of your choice and enjoy!

Berries Smoothie Bowl

INGREDIENTS

- ¾ cup fresh strawberries chopped
- ¾ cup fresh raspberries
- ¾ cup fresh blueberries
- ¾ cup fresh blackberries
- ¼ cup thick coconut milk

INSTRUCTIONS

In a high-speed blender, place all ingredients and blend until smooth.

Transfer the mixture to a Ninja CREAMi Dessert Tub.

Cover the tub with a lid and freeze for 24 hours.

After freezing, remove the lid from the tub and place it in the Outer Bowl. Install the Creamerizer Paddle.

Place the Outer Bowl on the motor base and lock it.

Turn **ON** the NINJA CREAMi and press the **SMOOTHIE BOWL** button.

Once the program is finished, release the Outer Bowl from the motor base and remove the lid.

Serve the smoothie bowl with the topping of your choice and enjoy!

Berry Walnut Smoothie Bowl

INGREDIENTS

- ½ cup blackberries
- ½ cup raspberries
- 1 handful of cauliflower
- 1 tbsp walnut butter
- 1 scoop vanilla protein powder
- ½ cup unsweetened almond milk

INSTRUCTIONS

In a high-speed blender, blend all ingredients and pulse until smooth.

Transfer the mixture to a Ninja CREAMi Dessert Tub.

Cover the tub with a lid and freeze for 24 hours.

After freezing, remove the lid from the tub and place it in the Outer Bowl. Install the Creamerizer Paddle.

Place the Outer Bowl on the motor base and lock it.

Turn **ON** the NINJA CREAMi and press the **SMOOTHIE BOWL** button.

Once the program is finished, release the Outer Bowl from the motor base and remove the lid.

Serve the smoothie bowl with the topping of your choice and enjoy!

Pecan Bread Smoothie Bowl

INGREDIENTS

- 1 cup strawberries
- 1 big handful of cauliflower
- 1 tbsp pecan butter
- 1 scoop vanilla protein powder
- ½ cup unsweetened almond milk
- ½ navel orange squeezed

INSTRUCTIONS

In a high-speed blender, blend all ingredients and pulse until smooth.

Transfer the mixture to a Ninja CREAMi Dessert Tub.

Cover the tub with a lid and freeze for 24 hours.

After freezing, remove the lid from the tub and place it in the Outer Bowl. Install the Creamerizer Paddle.

Place the Outer Bowl on the motor base and lock it.

Turn **ON** the NINJA CREAMi and press the **SMOOTHIE BOWL** button.

Once the program is finished, release the Outer Bowl from the motor base and remove the lid.

Serve the smoothie bowl with the topping of your choice and enjoy!

Blueberry Cashew Smoothie Bowl

INGREDIENTS

- 1 cup blueberries
- 1 big handful of cauliflower
- 1 tbsp raw cashew butter
- 1 scoop vanilla protein powder
- ½ cup unsweetened almond milk

INSTRUCTIONS

In a high-speed blender, blend all ingredients and pulse until smooth.

Transfer the mixture to a Ninja CREAMi Dessert Tub.

Cover the tub with a lid and freeze for 24 hours.

After freezing, remove the lid from the tub and place it in the Outer Bowl. Install the Creamerizer Paddle.

Place the Outer Bowl on the motor base and lock it.

Turn **ON** the NINJA CREAMi and press the **SMOOTHIE BOWL** button.

Once the program is finished, release the Outer Bowl from the motor base and remove the lid.

Serve the smoothie bowl with the topping of your choice and enjoy!

Avocado & Greens Smoothie Bowl

INGREDIENTS

- 1 cup pineapple
- 1 handful of cauliflower
- ½ small avocado
- 1 scoop vanilla protein powder
- ½ cup unsweetened almond
- 2 giant handfuls of spinach or kale

INSTRUCTIONS

In a high-speed blender, blend all ingredients and pulse until smooth.

Transfer the mixture to a Ninja CREAMi Dessert Tub.

Cover the tub with a lid and freeze for 24 hours.

After freezing, remove the lid from the tub and place it in the Outer Bowl. Install the Creamerizer Paddle.

Place the Outer Bowl on the motor base and lock it.

Turn **ON** the NINJA CREAMi and press the **SMOOTHIE BOWL** button.

Once the program is finished, release the Outer Bowl from the motor base and remove the lid.

Serve the smoothie bowl with the topping of your choice and enjoy!

Strawberry Avocado Smoothie Bowl

INGREDIENTS

- ½ large avocado, sliced
- ½ cup fresh strawberries, sliced
- ¼ cup fresh mint, roughly chopped
- 1 thumb-sized piece of fresh ginger, thinly sliced
- ½ tsp ground cinnamon
- ¼ tsp ground cardamom
- Juice of ¼ lime
- 2 cups unsweetened almond milk

INSTRUCTIONS

In a high-speed blender, blend all ingredients and pulse until smooth.

Transfer the mixture to a Ninja CREAMi Dessert Tub.

Cover the tub with a lid and freeze for 24 hours.

After freezing, remove the lid from the tub and place it in the Outer Bowl. Install the Creamerizer Paddle.

Place the Outer Bowl on the motor base and lock it.

Turn **ON** the NINJA CREAMi and press the **SMOOTHIE BOWL** button.

Once the program is finished, release the Outer Bowl from the motor base and remove the lid.

Serve the smoothie bowl with the topping of your choice and enjoy!

Coffee Smoothie Bowl

INGREDIENTS

- ¼ cup instant coffee powder
- 1 scoop vanilla protein powder
- 2 cups unsweetened vanilla almond milk

INSTRUCTIONS

Whisk all ingredients in a large mixing bowl until well combined and the coffee is dissolved.

Transfer the mixture to a Ninja CREAMi Dessert Tub.

Cover the tub with a lid and freeze for 24 hours.

After freezing, remove the lid from the tub and place it in the Outer Bowl. Install the Creamerizer Paddle.

Place the Outer Bowl on the motor base and lock it.

Turn **ON** the NINJA CREAMi and press the **SMOOTHIE BOWL** button.

Once the program is finished, release the Outer Bowl from the motor base and remove the lid.

Serve the smoothie bowl with the topping of your choice and enjoy!

SORBETS

Peach Sorbet

INGREDIENTS

- 16 oz peach slices

INSTRUCTIONS

Pour the peach into a Ninja CREAMi Dessert Tub.

Cover the tub with a lid and freeze for 24 hours.

After freezing, remove the lid from the tub and place it in the Outer Bowl. Install the Creamerizer Paddle.

Place the tub in the Outer Bowl. Install the Creamerizer Paddle.

Place the Outer Bowl on the motor base and lock it.

Turn **ON** the NINJA CREAMi and press the **SORBET** button.

Once the program is finished, release the Outer Bowl from the motor base and remove the lid.

If the sorbet is crumbly, reattach the lid and place the bowl on the motor base and lock it. Press the **RE-SPIN** button.

Once the sorbet is at the right consistency, serve and enjoy!

Pineapple Sorbet

INGREDIENTS

- 1 can (20 oz) pineapple chunks in juice

INSTRUCTIONS

Pour the can of pineapple chunks with juice into a Ninja CREAMi Dessert Tub.

Cover the tub with a lid and freeze for 24 hours.

After freezing, remove the lid from the tub and place it in the Outer Bowl. Install the Creamerizer Paddle.

Place the tub in the Outer Bowl. Install the Creamerizer Paddle.

Place the Outer Bowl on the motor base and lock it.

Turn **ON** the NINJA CREAMi and press the **SORBET** button.

Once the program is finished, release the Outer Bowl from the motor base and remove the lid.

If the sorbet is crumbly, reattach the lid and place the bowl on the motor base and lock it. Press the **RE-SPIN** button.

Once the sorbet is at the right consistency, serve and enjoy!

Orange Sorbet

INGREDIENTS

- 20 oz canned mandarin orange slices, in their own juice

INSTRUCTIONS

Pour the mandarin oranges and juice into a Ninja CREAMi Dessert Tub.

Cover the tub with a lid and freeze for 24 hours.

After freezing, remove the lid from the tub and place it in the Outer Bowl. Install the Creamerizer Paddle.

Place the tub in the Outer Bowl. Install the Creamerizer Paddle.

Place the Outer Bowl on the motor base and lock it.

Turn **ON** the NINJA CREAMi and press the **SORBET** button.

Once the program is finished, release the Outer Bowl from the motor base and remove the lid.

If the sorbet is crumbly, reattach the lid and place the bowl on the motor base and lock it. Press the **RE-SPIN** button.

Once the sorbet is at the right consistency, serve and enjoy!

Mango Sorbet

INGREDIENTS

- 16 oz mango slices

INSTRUCTIONS

Pour the mango slices into a Ninja CREAMi Dessert Tub.

Cover the tub with a lid and freeze for 24 hours.

After freezing, remove the lid from the tub and place it in the Outer Bowl. Install the Creamerizer Paddle.

Place the tub in the Outer Bowl. Install the Creamerizer Paddle.

Place the Outer Bowl on the motor base and lock it.

Turn **ON** the NINJA CREAMi and press the **SORBET** button.

Once the program is finished, release the Outer Bowl from the motor base and remove the lid.

If the sorbet is crumbly, reattach the lid and place the bowl on the motor base and lock it. Press the **RE-SPIN** button.

Once the sorbet is at the right consistency, serve and enjoy!

Lemon Sorbet

INGREDIENTS

- 1 cup warm water
- ¼ cup monk fruit sweetener
- ½ cup lemon juice

INSTRUCTIONS

Mix the warm water and sweetener in a small bowl. Stir until the sweetener is dissolved. Stir in the lemon juice.

Pour the mixture into a Ninja CREAMi Dessert Tub.

Cover the tub with a lid and freeze for 24 hours.

After freezing, remove the lid from the tub and place it in the Outer Bowl. Install the Creamerizer Paddle.

Place the tub in the Outer Bowl. Install the Creamerizer Paddle.

Place the Outer Bowl on the motor base and lock it.

Turn **ON** the NINJA CREAMi and press the **SORBET** button.

Once the program is finished, release the Outer Bowl from the motor base and remove the lid.

If the sorbet is crumbly, reattach the lid and place the bowl on the motor base and lock it. Press the **RE-SPIN** button.

Once the sorbet is at the right consistency, serve and enjoy!

Strawberry Sorbet

INGREDIENTS

- 3 cups fresh strawberries quartered
- 1 tbsp monk fruit sweetener

INSTRUCTIONS

In a medium bowl, mix together the strawberries and sweetener. Using the back of a fork, smash the strawberries until they begin to release their juice. Stir everything together until the sweetener is dissolved.

Pour the strawberry mixture into a Ninja CREAMi Dessert Tub.

Cover the tub with a lid and freeze for 24 hours.

After freezing, remove the lid from the tub and place it in the Outer Bowl. Install the Creamerizer Paddle.

Place the tub in the Outer Bowl. Install the Creamerizer Paddle.

Place the Outer Bowl on the motor base and lock it.

Turn **ON** the NINJA CREAMi and press the **SORBET** button.

Once the program is finished, release the Outer Bowl from the motor base and remove the lid.

If the sorbet is crumbly, reattach the lid and place the bowl on the motor base and lock it. Press the **RE-SPIN** button.

Once the sorbet is at the right consistency, serve and enjoy!

Raspberry Sorbet

INGREDIENTS

- 3 cups fresh raspberries
- 3 tbsp monk fruit sweetener

INSTRUCTIONS

In a medium bowl, mix together the raspberries and sweetener. Using the back of a fork smash the raspberries until they begin to release their juice. Stir everything together until the sweetener is dissolved.

Pour the raspberry mixture into a Ninja CREAMi Dessert Tub.

Cover the tub with a lid and freeze for 24 hours.

After freezing, remove the lid from the tub and place it in the Outer Bowl. Install the Creamerizer Paddle.

Place the tub in the Outer Bowl. Install the Creamerizer Paddle.

Place the Outer Bowl on the motor base and lock it.

Turn **ON** the NINJA CREAMi and press the **SORBET** button.

Once the program is finished, release the Outer Bowl from the motor base and remove the lid.

If the sorbet is crumbly, reattach the lid and place the bowl on the motor base and lock it. Press the **RE-SPIN** button.

Once the sorbet is at the right consistency, serve and enjoy!

Mojito Sorbet

INGREDIENTS

- ½ cup water
- ¼ cup mint leaves
- 1 teaspoon grated lime zest
- ½ cup freshly squeezed lime juice
- ¾ cup citrus-flavored sparkling water
- 3 tbsp monk fruit sweetener

INSTRUCTIONS

In a medium bowl, place all ingredients and mix until sweetener is dissolved.

Pour the mixture into a Ninja CREAMi Dessert Tub.

Cover the tub with a lid and freeze for 24 hours.

After freezing, remove the lid from the tub and place it in the Outer Bowl. Install the Creamerizer Paddle.

Place the tub in the Outer Bowl. Install the Creamerizer Paddle.

Place the Outer Bowl on the motor base and lock it.

Turn **ON** the NINJA CREAMi and press the **SORBET** button.

Once the program is finished, release the Outer Bowl from the motor base and remove the lid.

If the sorbet is crumbly, reattach the lid and place the bowl on the motor base and lock it. Press the **RE-SPIN** button.

Once the sorbet is at the right consistency, serve and enjoy!

Kiwi Sorbet

INGREDIENTS

- 2 cups sliced strawberries
- 4 kiwis chopped
- ¼ cup water

INSTRUCTIONS

In a high-speed blender, pulse all the ingredients until the mixture is smooth.

Pour the mixture into a Ninja CREAMi Dessert Tub.

Cover the tub with a lid and freeze for 24 hours.

After freezing, remove the lid from the tub and place it in the Outer Bowl. Install the Creamerizer Paddle.

Place the tub in the Outer Bowl. Install the Creamerizer Paddle.

Place the Outer Bowl on the motor base and lock it.

Turn **ON** the NINJA CREAMi and press the **SORBET** button.

Once the program is finished, release the Outer Bowl from the motor base and remove the lid.

If the sorbet is crumbly, reattach the lid and place the bowl on the motor base and lock it. Press the **RE-SPIN** button.

Once the sorbet is at the right consistency, serve and enjoy!